OECD Development Policy Tools

The Role of Sovereign and Strategic Investment Funds in the Low-carbon Transition

This work is published under the responsibility of the Secretary-General of the OECD. The opinions expressed and arguments employed herein do not necessarily reflect the official views of the member countries of the OECD or its Development Centre.

This document, as well as any data and map included herein, are without prejudice to the status of or sovereignty over any territory, to the delimitation of international frontiers and boundaries and to the name of any territory, city or area.

Please cite this publication as:
OECD (2020), *The Role of Sovereign and Strategic Investment Funds in the Low-carbon Transition*, OECD Development Policy Tools, OECD Publishing, Paris, *https://doi.org/10.1787/ddfd6a9f-en*.

ISBN 978-92-64-44720-2 (print)
ISBN 978-92-64-68075-3 (pdf)

OECD Development Policy Tools
ISSN 2518-6248 (print)
ISSN 2518-3702 (online)

Photo credits: Cover design by Aida Buendía (OECD Development Centre) based on images from © Der_Wolf/Shutterstock.com.

Corrigenda to publications may be found on line at: *www.oecd.org/about/publishing/corrigenda.htm*.
© OECD 2020

The use of this work, whether digital or print, is governed by the Terms and Conditions to be found at *http://www.oecd.org/termsandconditions*.

Foreword

This publication was prepared by the OECD Development Centre, within the framework of the Policy Dialogue on Natural Resource-based Development. A preliminary version of the publication was presented and discussed at the Thirteenth Plenary Meeting of the Policy Dialogue, held on 25-26 November 2019 at the OECD in Paris. The publication is a product of the Policy Dialogue's Work Stream 2 on Revenue Management and Spending. It continues the line of work started with the Policy Dialogue's previous publication in the OECD Development Policy Tools series, "Using Extractive Revenues for Sustainable Development".

Acknowledgements

This report was authored by Håvard Halland, Senior Economist at the Natural Resources for Development Unit, OECD Development Centre. It was prepared under the guidance and supervision of Lahra Liberti, Head of the Natural Resources for Development Unit, OECD Development Centre.

Several persons provided information crucial to the drafting of the report. The author is in that regard grateful to Duncan Bonfield, CEO of the International Forum of Sovereign Funds; Ben Caldecott, founding Director of the Oxford Sustainable Finance Programme and Associate Professor of the University of Oxford Smith School of Enterprise and the Environment; Elizabeth Harnett, Lead, Future of Engagement, Oxford Sustainable Finance Programme; Mohamed Jameel Al Ramahi, CEO of Masdar; Frédéric Samama, Deputy Global Head of Institutional and Sovereign Clients at Amundi; and Stephen Worsley, Acting Head of Corporate Communications at Masdar. The author is also grateful to participants at the 13th Plenary of the Policy Dialogue on Natural Resource-based Development, for their feedback and comments.

The author would like to thank OECD colleagues, in particular Lahra Liberti for her guidance during the drafting process, and Federico Bonaglia, Deputy Director of the OECD Development Centre, for overall direction on publications. The report has benefited from administrative support by Parissa Nahani, and Delphine Grandrieux supported the publication process.

Table of contents

Foreword 3

Acknowledgements 4

Abbreviations and acronyms 7

Abstract 9

Executive summary 10

1 Introduction 12

2 The relevance of sovereign funds and SIFs to climate finance 13
    Institutional mandate 13
    Investment policy 14

3 Climate risks and opportunities for sovereign funds and SIFs 15

4 The current role of sovereign funds and SIFs in climate finance 17
    Sovereign funds 22
    Strategic investment funds 24

5 How sovereign funds and SIFs can play a stronger role in the low-carbon transition 26
    Sovereign funds 26
    Strategic investment funds 32
    Collaboration between sovereign funds and SIFs: Harnessing their potential for enhanced climate finance and action 34

6 Conclusions 35

Notes 37

References 38

FIGURES

Figure 1. Sovereign funds and SIFs' climate alignment at different levels 19

TABLES

Table 1. Sovereign fund and SIF participation in climate-related investor initiatives   23

Abbreviations and acronyms

ADIA	Abu Dhabi Investment Authority
AUM	Assets under management
BPIFrance	Banque publique d'investissement (France)
CCPIB	Canada Pension Plan Investment Board
CDC	Caisse des dépôts et consignations (France)
ESG	Environmental, social, and governance
EU	European Union
FONSIS	Fonds d'Investissement Stratégique du Sénégal
GDP	Gross domestic product
GPFG	Government Pension Fund Global (Norway)
IFRS	International Financial Reporting Standards
IPCC	Intergovernmental Panel on Climate Change
ISIF	Ireland Strategic Investment Fund
KIA	Kuwait Investment Authority
NBIM	Norges Bank Investment Management
NIF	Nigeria Infrastructure Fund
NIIF	National Investment and Infrastructure Fund (India)
NOK	Norwegian Krone
NZSF	New Zealand Superannuation Fund
OTPP	Ontario Teachers' Pension Plan
PIF	Public Investment Fund (Saudi Arabia)
PIH	Permanent income hypothesis

PKA	Pensionskassernes Administration A/S (Denmark)
QIA	Qatar Investment Authority
SIFs	Strategic investment funds
SMEs	Small and medium-sized enterprises
SRF	Silk Road Fund
Sovereign funds	Sovereign funds
SWFI	Sovereign wealth fund Institute
TCFD	Task Force on Climate-Related Disclosures
USD	United States Dollars
UNCTAD	United Nations Conference on Trade and Development

Abstract

Sovereign funds manage a large share of the world's invested capital. The action or inaction of these funds on climate finance is of crucial importance to the world's ability to reach the goals of the Paris Agreement and restrain global warming to below 2 degrees Celsius. However, sovereign funds have so far played a very limited role in climate finance. This report provides guidance on how governments can support their sovereign funds in becoming climate-aligned commercial investors. The establishment of synergies between sovereign funds and strategic investment funds can help scale up investments in clean-energy infrastructure.

Executive summary

Sovereign funds,[1] many of which are funded by natural-resource revenues, hold about USD 8.2 trillion of assets under management. Sovereign funds' action or inaction on climate finance is therefore of crucial importance to the world's ability to reach the goals of the Paris Agreement and limit global warming to below 2 degrees Celsius. At the same time, climate change could significantly increase the risk to sovereign funds' portfolios. A review of the literature indicates that climate risk could be under-priced by financial markets, while several studies indicate that low-carbon investment portfolios perform well. Climate change thus brings investment opportunities as well as risk. Addressing climate risk and taking account of climate-related opportunities, is part of sovereign funds' fiduciary responsibilities to citizens and to their governments.

Sovereign funds are commercial investors, with a fiduciary duty to maximise risk-adjusted returns according to their mandate and save for future generations. Sovereign funds' climate-related objectives remain largely aspirational, in spite of important recent initiatives. Many sovereign funds are largely passive with regard to climate risk and climate impact. With respect to climate risk, Norway's Government Pension Fund Global, and the New Zealand Superannuation Fund are among the few sovereign funds that are known to assess such risk systematically in their portfolio companies. Regarding climate impact, on average less than 1% of sovereign funds' investments go to low-carbon solutions. Furthermore, few sovereign funds disclose information about their climate policies and strategies, and few have adopted climate-focused active ownership policies to reduce the carbon footprints of their portfolios.

Sovereign funds receive their mandates from their governments. They are unlikely to take climate-related action on their own, and unless governments provide them with the resources necessary to meet associated costs. These costs may include the upgrading of mandates, governance structures, investment strategy, partnerships and risk-management frameworks, as well as recurrent costs associated with operating as active climate-aligned owners.

Sovereign funds can undertake climate-related engagement with their portfolio companies either directly or through their asset managers. Sovereign funds that seek to climate-align their operations, and that outsource most or all of their asset management to external asset management companies, should seek to select, monitor and oversee asset managers not only based on financial results but also based on climate impact.

To achieve higher allocations to low-carbon solutions, many sovereign funds would need to undertake major investments in capacity building – at the levels of board, management and staff, and across several areas. This includes i) capacity to engage with portfolio companies on climate-related issues; ii) capacity to select and monitor asset managers based on their climate-related performance, as well as – for the stronger sovereign funds – iii) capacity to invest directly in low-carbon infrastructure.

Well functioning strategic investment funds (SIFs) already have many of the characteristics required to play an important role in the low-carbon transition. SIFs differ from sovereign funds by having "double bottom line" objectives of financial returns combined with the achievement of policy goals. SIFs are domestically focused, and they seek to mobilise private capital for investment in priority sectors and regions. SIFs can contribute to the low-carbon transition by providing equity and other forms of investment capital to sectors and stages of the investment process where the private sector does not invest by itself. However, SIFs are very small compared to sovereign funds, and would need far larger amounts of capital to contribute meaningfully to the low-carbon transition.

Sovereign funds and SIFs are complementary in several ways, and the synergies between them could be further exploited. Sovereign funds could benefit from collaborating more closely with SIFs that already have many of the skills required for playing an important role in climate finance, as well as with pension funds that have built the capacity for direct infrastructure investment. For SIFs, collaboration with sovereign funds would provide an opportunity to scale their investments in low-carbon infrastructure and other climate-related assets. This could be done by channelling part of sovereign funds' capital through SIFs, or by setting up joint investment platforms with SIFs to pool resources and expertise to co-invest in green infrastructure.

1 Introduction

Sovereign funds hold a significant share of global invested capital, with assets worth about USD 8.2 trillion (Sovereign Wealth Fund Institute, 2020[1]). They control about 8% of all listed equities worldwide (Capapé and Santiváñez, 2017[2]). By way of comparison, pension funds, the largest group of institutional investors, globally hold USD 45 trillion (WillisTowersWatson, 2019[3]). There is a close connection between many sovereign funds and natural resource wealth. 57% of sovereign funds are capitalised from natural-resource revenues, mainly from oil and gas, with the remaining 43% being funded from non-commodity sources such as foreign exchange reserves and fiscal savings rules (Capape, 2017[4]). Many sovereign funds, especially in resource-rich countries, are large relative to their home economies. In 2015, 16 sovereign funds managed assets equivalent to more than 50% of their country's GDP (Ossowski and Halland, 2016[5]). At the same time, the capital held by sovereign funds is highly concentrated, with the largest 20 sovereign funds controlling about 90% of total sovereign fund assets (Capape, 2017[4]). The actions of a small number of large sovereign funds could thus have very important implications for the low-carbon transition.

The permanent income hypothesis (PIH) has for long been seen as the benchmark for the role of sovereign funds in the fiscal policy of resource-rich countries. According to the PIH, a country should save enough of its resource revenues (in a sovereign fund) to maintain a permanent income from the return on invested capital towards the indefinite future. However, over the last 6-8 years policy makers and academics have increasingly recognised that, in capital-starved countries, the returns to investing resource revenues domestically could be higher than from investing these revenues abroad – in both economic and financial terms (van den Bremer and van der Ploeg, 2013[6]). In contexts where capacity for high-quality investment management is available, and investment decisions can be implemented free from political influence, within strong corporate governance frameworks, this shift in attitudes has opened up opportunities for the domestic investment of resource revenues through SIFs.

A number of emerging markets and developing economies (EMDEs) have established SIFs, including, among others, Gabon, Ghana, India, Malaysia, Morocco, Nigeria, the Philippines, Senegal, Rwanda and Viet Nam. The level of climate alignment of these SIFs will determine the ability of their countries to reduce e greenhouse-gas emissions and achieve their intended nationally determined contributions (INDC) under the Paris agreement.

This report is structured as follows: Section 2 explains the relevance of sovereign funds and SIFs for climate finance. Section 3 considers the effect of climate risk and opportunities on sovereign funds and SIFs. Section 4 discusses the current role of sovereign funds and SIFs in climate finance, whereas Section 5 considers barriers that prevent sovereign funds and SIFs from adopting a more proactive role in the low-carbon transition, and how these barriers can be addressed. Section 6 concludes.

2 The relevance of sovereign funds and SIFs to climate finance

The combination of increased climate risk and declining revenues from fossil fuels will significantly affect the sovereign funds of fossil fuel-exporting countries. At the same time, the sheer magnitude of sovereign funds' capital, and their role as investors in companies across the globe, means that these investment funds are necessarily significant actors in the low-carbon transition (OECD, 2019[7]). Conversely, while the actions of sovereign funds have an impact on climate change, climate change also has an impact on sovereign funds through increased risk. Sovereign funds are diversified across a broad range of sectors and geographies. Climate risk, from which no sector is immune, is therefore likely to affect their portfolios significantly. Whether sovereign funds choose to take a leading role as climate-aligned investors, or remain passive, their actions will have crucial implications for the world's ability to address climate change, and for the risk-adjusted value of their own portfolios.

Whereas the importance of sovereign funds to climate finance arises from their scale, SIFs are relevant due to their growing track record as commercial, yet policy-driven investors. Upwards of 30 SIFs have so far been established, most of them after the 2008 financial crisis. Several others are being planned or considered. Examples of SIFs include Bpifrance, the Ireland Strategic Investment Fund, Khazakhstan's Baiterek, the Nigeria Infrastructure Fund (NIF), Senegal's *Fonds d'Investissement Stratégiques* (FONSIS), and India's National Investment and Infrastructure Fund (NIIF). The EU's Marguerite Fund and the Africa Renewable Energy Fund are examples of SIFs that operate at the regional level.

Most SIFs are smaller than sovereign funds by orders of magnitude. The largest infrastructure-focused SIF, India's NIIF, seeks a capitalisation of USD 6 billion, whereas the largest sovereign fund, Norway's Government Pension Fund Global (GPFG) holds assets worth nearly USD 1 trillion, or about 170 times more than the NIIF. The exception to this rule is highly diversified sovereign funds with a strategic (SIF) component, which invest both abroad and at home. This includes Mubadala Investment Company (USD 369 billion in assets under management [AUM]), Malaysia's Khazanah Nasional Berhad (USD 37 billion AUM), and Bahrain's Mumtalakat (USD 15.5 billion AUM). These funds have portfolios that comprise foreign as well as domestic assets, but still invest with a "double bottom line" objective of contributing to the development of their national economies. For example, Gulf funds have played an important role in realising the ambition of building technology and aerospace sectors in their home countries. However, while SIFs are policy-driven investors, their focus on commercial returns enhances the integrity of the investment process, and reduces the potential for political interference in the investment process (OECD, 2019[8]) (Gelb, Tordo and Halland, 2014[9]) (Halland, Noel and Tordo, 2016[10]).

Institutional mandate

Whereas sovereign funds' policy objectives are to save for future generations, with a possible fiscal stabilisation component, strategic investment funds (SIFs) are mandated to invest directly in priority sectors of national and regional economies. Many SIFs focus primarily on the development of national infrastructure, including clean-energy infrastructure, or on the financing of small and medium-sized enterprises (SMEs). Beyond their role as commercial investors, SIFs are also instruments of economic and financial policy. These state-sponsored funds invest mainly domestically, under a "double bottom line" mandate of commercial returns and economic, environmental, or social impact – or even a "triple bottom line" that also includes the mobilisation of private capital for investment in priority sectors of national economies. Several governments have set up SIFs with a mandate to catalyse private financing for new infrastructure projects, including clean-energy infrastructure (OECD, 2019[8]). However, SIFs hold only a tiny fraction of the capital that sovereign funds control, and their capacity to drive global change is therefore at present very limited.

Investment policy

Contrary to SIFs, sovereign funds do not have a "double bottom line". As commercial investors, sovereign funds seek to maximise the risk-adjusted returns on their investments and do not invest domestically. Sovereign funds invest mainly abroad, in foreign-currency denominated financial assets.[2] Sovereign funds are well placed to act as long-term investors. Whereas the share of capital that sovereign funds hold for fiscal stabilisation purposes is largely irrelevant to climate finance, since it needs to be held in liquid assets, capital that sovereign funds invest for the long term, can be used to seek risk-adjusted returns in low-carbon assets.

Since sovereign funds do not have short-term liabilities, and have a policy mandate to guard wealth for future generations, these funds are in a position to seek additional returns arising from long-term investment opportunities (Singh Bachher, Dixon and Monk, 2017[11]). Sovereign funds' long-term investment horizon allows them to seek attractive commercial returns from investing in long-lived illiquid assets, including commercial clean-energy infrastructure. This differs from much of the global equity market, where many investors have shorter investment horizons and seek to avoid illiquid assets.

Sovereign funds' climate-related policies need to be consistent not only with their financial objectives, but also with their fiduciary duties and macroeconomic functions. In fossil fuel-exporting countries, this typically includes mitigation of exchange rate appreciation ("Dutch disease"), fiscal stabilisation objectives, as well as long-term savings objectives. Reflecting this type of objectives, sovereign funds' investment in low-carbon assets should take place abroad and on commercial terms. Another reason that these funds should not invest domestically is the risk of political influence on investment decisions.

Domestic investment should be reserved for SIFs, and for sovereign funds with a clear SIF function, where safeguards and capabilities appropriate to SIFs can be established. A number of SIFs have the capacity to undertake project development for new "greenfield" infrastructure. Recently, an increasing number of sovereign funds have acquired the capacity to undertake direct equity investment (Capape, 2017[4]). For now, this is with a view to generating profits in the technology sector, but it does demonstrate that, if given the right incentives, sovereign funds can build the skills to become direct equity investors.

3 Climate risks and opportunities for sovereign funds and SIFs

Climate change generates risk that will affect the portfolios of sovereign funds and SIFs. Although vulnerability to climate change varies considerably between geographies and sectors, climate change generates increased risk across sectors and asset classes. The risks take three main forms:

1. Physical risk is the risk of physical damage to real assets, caused by changing precipitation patterns and increased frequency of extreme weather events such as floods, draughts, storms and heat waves. Weather-related damage to real assets could cause portfolio companies to cease or modify operations, affecting their valuation.

2. Transition risk refers to the likelihood of significant changes in asset valuations during the transition to a low-carbon economy. This includes the risk of stranded assets in high-emissions sectors such as coal, oil and gas. The low-carbon transition could shift the competitive advantage of entire regions and sectors, affecting investor portfolios and broad financial stability (Carney, 2015[12]) (Caldecott and Harnett, n.d.[13])

3. Liability risk could arise from failures to disclose and manage climate risk, and liabilities for companies that have contributed significantly to carbon emissions.

The impact of physical risks and transition risks depends on the magnitude of future temperature increase. In a "business as usual" scenario, with limited efforts to combat climate change and a global average temperature increase of 2.6-4.8 degrees Celsius, physical impacts are likely to be catastrophic. Physical risks will then dominate. In a scenario of ambitious climate policies, and a below 1.5 degrees Celsius global average temperature increase, transition risk is likely to dominate, with less physical risk. Either way, sovereign funds' portfolios are likely to be profoundly affected by climate change (Caldecott and Harnett, n.d.[13]) (Caldecott, 2018[14]).

According to (BNP Paribas, 2019[15]), the effect of carbon pricing on firm profits and equity value could be material as soon as 2020-25. In an aggressive carbon-pricing scenario, companies in the utilities, basic materials, energy and industrial sectors may cease to be viable operating entities. In these cases, the portfolio impact is therefore potentially 100% loss of the exposure.

Climate change will create winners as well as losers, as the low-carbon transition generates investment opportunities across geographies, sectors and asset classes. This is likely to increase global demand for capital (Carney, 2016[16]) (Caldecott and Harnett, n.d.[13]). Companies that contribute to the low-carbon transition, or are otherwise able to position themselves in the context of a changing climate, are likely to see their valuations rise – in turn having an impact on the portfolios of sovereign funds and SIFs.

Investment opportunities are likely to continue arising in low-carbon infrastructure, and in low-carbon technology. In the infrastructure sectors, global needs compatible with low-carbon and climate resilient development amount to USD 7 trillion per year for the next 15 years, of which USD 3.9 trillion in developing countries (OECD, 2018[17]). The investment gap for developing countries, or difference with the current level of around USD 1.4 trillion, is estimated at USD 2.5 trillion per year (UNCTAD, 2014[18]). This is broadly consistent with the findings of the 2018 special report of the Intergovernmental Panel on Climate Change (IPCC), which estimates investment needs for the global energy system at 2.5% of world GDP between 2016 and 2035. By comparison, total official overseas development assistance in 2018 amounted to USD 153 billion (OECD, 2019[19]), or about 6% of the investment gap for developing countries. A significant share of the infrastructure will need to be built on commercial terms, and sovereign funds and SIFs that manage to position themselves as infrastructure investors will be well placed to invest in commercial infrastructure projects.

4 The current role of sovereign funds and SIFs in climate finance

The most direct way of assessing the level of climate alignment of sovereign funds and SIFs is by focusing on the climate impact of these funds' portfolio assets. A sovereign fund or a SIF, like any other investment organisation, can reduce its carbon footprint by: i) investing in low-carbon assets and technological innovation, ii) excluding or divesting from inefficient high-carbon ones, and iii) by working with portfolio companies to reduce their emissions through the adoption of renewable energy, energy efficiency measures, or clean-energy technology.

Climate-aligned asset management is supported by climate-aligned investment processes. A second, complementary, option for assessing a sovereign fund's or SIF's climate alignment is therefore to focus on the investment process that underpins the evolution of its portfolio. Two frameworks are particularly relevant for sovereign funds and SIFs. The Task Force on Climate-Related Disclosures (TCFD) captures climate alignment of investment processes by the four concepts of governance, strategy, risk management, and metrics and targets. The One Planet Sovereign Wealth Fund Group (Box 1), refers to the climate-aligned investment process by the concepts of alignment, ownership and integration. Whereas the TCFD framework refers mainly to investor organisations' internal processes, the One Planet framework focuses on the climate alignment of a sovereign fund's mandate, interaction with portfolio companies, as well as process.

For externally managed assets, sovereign funds can seek to have their asset managers undertake low-carbon investment, emissions-related engagement with portfolio companies, as well as exclusion and divestment from inefficient high-carbon assets. Sophisticated sovereign funds, such as Norway's Government Pension Fund Global (GPFG), engage directly with externally managed portfolio companies on climate issues, whereas many other sovereign funds leave portfolio company engagement to their asset managers. Such engagement may include support for energy efficiency measures, less carbon-intensive production and value-chains, and the adoption of low-emission energy sources. In recognition of the critical role of asset managers in implementing sovereign funds' climate-related objectives, the One Planet Sovereign Wealth Fund Group recently established a corresponding One Planet Asset Manager Initiative (Box 1).

> **Box 1. One Planet Sovereign Wealth Fund Working Group**
>
> The One Planet Sovereign Wealth Fund Working Group (SWF Group) was established in 2017, following the 2015 Paris Agreement to mitigate the effects of climate change. The SWF group was one of several One Planet initiatives initiated by French President Emmanuel Macron. The SWF Group consists of six sovereign funds, which collectively hold more than USD 3 trillion worth of assets.
>
> The One Planet SWF Group was established in recognition of sovereign funds' role as influential, long-term investors, and their potential to promote long-term value creation and sustainable market outcomes. The Group was established "to accelerate efforts to integrate financial risks and opportunities

related to climate change in the management of large, long-term asset pools." The Group seeks to enhance sovereign funds' capacity to address climate risk, and is not explicitly an instrument of climate policy.

In July 2018, the One Planet SWF Group published the One Planet SWF Framework. The objective of the Framework is to promote the integration of climate change analysis, and climate-related risk and opportunities, in the management of large, long-term and diversified asset pools. The Framework aims to "foster a shared understanding of key principles, methodologies, and indicators related to climate change; identify climate-related risk and opportunities; and enhance their investment decision-making frameworks to better inform their priorities as investors and participants in financial markets".

The Framework is based on three principles:

- Principle 1: Alignment – Build climate change considerations, which are aligned with the Sovereign fund's investment horizons, into decision making.
- Principle 2: Ownership – Encourage companies to address material climate change issues in their governance, business strategy and planning, risk management and public reporting to promote value creation.
- Principle 3: Integration – Integrate the consideration of climate change-related risks and opportunities into investment management, to improve the resilience of long-term investment portfolios.

Members of the One Planet SWF Group recognise that their climate-related efforts would need to be supported by their asset managers, and in July 2019 established the One Planet Asset Managers Initiative. The initiative includes eight global asset managers, with a combined USD 15 trillion of assets under management, who have committed to support the implementation of the Framework.

In July 2019, the One Planet SWF Group also announced the formation of the One Planet SWF Research Forum, in partnership with the Global Research Alliance for Sustainable Finance and Investment. The Research Forum aims to support the One Planet funds by "identifying and facilitating rigorous and impactful research projects relevant to the implementation of the One Planet SWF Framework, as well as providing training and capacity building for One Planet SWF Members".

The One Planet SWF Group founding members are Abu Dhabi Investment Authority, Kuwait Investment Authority, New Zealand Superannuation Fund, Norges Bank Investment Management, Public Investment Fund (Saudi Arabia), and Qatar Investment Authority.

Source: One Planet SWF Group website.

As illustrated in Figure 1, the level of climate alignment of a sovereign fund or a SIF can thus be assessed i) at the asset level; ii) at the intermediary or asset manager level; and/or iii) at the portfolio and process level. This section discusses the current role of sovereign funds and SIFs in climate finance, at these three different levels. The first part of the section considers sovereign funds, whereas the second part looks at SIFs.

Figure 1. Sovereign funds and SIFs' climate alignment at different levels

Impact level		Climate impact		
Asset level	EU Taxonomy	Investing in low-carbon assets, including technological innovation	Divesting from inefficient high-carbon assets	Reduce carbon footprint of portfolio companies
Asset manager level	One Planet SWF Asset Managers	Selection and monitoring of asset managers based on climate criteria		
Policy and process level	One Planet SWF	Alignment	Ownership	Integration
	TCFD	Governance	Strategy	Risk management	Metrics & targets

The climate impact of a sovereign fund's equity portfolio is the aggregate climate impact of the activities undertaken by the sovereign fund's portfolio companies, weighted by the sovereign fund's equity share in each of these companies. The most direct way of assessing the sovereign fund's role as an equity investor is therefore to calculate the weighted aggregate portfolio impact according to a defined standard – such as the new EU Taxonomy (Box 4). The climate assessment of a sovereign fund's fixed-income portfolios is facilitated by the ongoing consolidation of green bonds standards. This includes the EU's new Green Bonds standard, which seeks to provide a common standard for EU countries.

According to (Bloomberg NEF, 2019[20])(2019) global clean-energy investment has reached USD 300 billion annually for the past five years. However, very little of this investment comes from sovereign funds. According to (Capape, 2017[4]), the total value of sovereign funds' climate-aligned investment during the three-year period 2014-16 was USD 11 billion. This includes not only sovereign funds' investments in clean energy, but also green debt funds and platforms, green infrastructure, green agriculture and green startups. The total value is equivalent to about 0.15% of sovereign funds' total assets under management. Another estimate suggests that sovereign funds' green investments grew from zero in 2006 to about 1% of the value of all reported deals in 2015 – with an uptick to 3.5% in 2016, driven by a small number of large deals (OECD, 2016[21]).

Sovereign funds' low allocation to climate-aligned investments is reflective of these funds' low allocation to infrastructure in general. In 2017, sovereign funds completed 28 direct investments in infrastructure, for a total value of USD 8 billion (International Forum of Sovereign Wealth Funds, 2019[22]), or about 0.1% of the value of total assets under management by sovereign funds. Sovereign funds' small allocation to low-carbon assets also reflects common practice amongst institutional investors overall. The (Asset Owners Disclosure Project, 2018[23]) finds that large pension fund portfolios on average have only 1% allocation to low-carbon solutions, although there are exceptions with low-carbon allocations of up to 6%.

One significant exception to the rule of low sovereign fund investment in low-carbon assets is the United Arab Emirates' Mubadala Investment Company, a sovereign fund that through its fully owned subsidiary Masdar has developed a high level of capacity to invest in clean-energy infrastructure (Box 2).

> **Box 2. Sovereign fund investment in new clean-energy infrastructure: The case of Masdar**
>
> The Mubadala Investment Company is among the very few sovereign funds that invest significantly in new, "greenfield", clean-energy infrastructure. Mubadala undertakes this type of investment through Masdar, its fully owned subsidiary. Masdar is a private joint-stock company incorporated in Abu Dhabi. The company seeks to support the diversification of Abu Dhabi's energy sources and economy, while delivering financial returns to its owner, Mubadala. Masdar was established to invest in commercially viable renewable-energy infrastructure projects in the MENA region and globally, and in sustainable urban development in Abu Dhabi. Given its comparatively small home market in the United Arab Emirates, Masdar has since the beginning pursued investments abroad. This has allowed it to acquire the necessary scale and competencies to operate at a global scale.
>
> Masdar is both a developer and an operator of utility-scale renewable energy projects. It has the in-house capability to conduct end-to-end project development for greenfield infrastructure, but may also engage later in the project lifecycle. This could be at the time of financial close, when it would participate in the late-stage negotiations and construction management. Since it was established in 2006, Masdar has invested USD 4.5 billion in renewable energy projects, which have a combined value of USD 14.3 billion. The company participates in some of the world's largest clean-energy infrastructure projects, including the London Array in the United Kingdom – which when built was the world's largest offshore wind project.
>
> Masdar's business model seeks to commercialise novel technologies in solar power, wind energy, sustainable real estate, and waste-to-energy. Whereas Masdar initially prioritised markets that had government commitments to decarbonisation and renewable energy, the maturing of the renewable energy sector means that business fundamentals are now more important. This includes supply and demand, regulatory regimes, political stability, auxiliary infrastructure, and counterparty risk. Masdar's target IRRs, based on the risk profile of each asset, are primarily driven by considerations that include:
>
> - Geography – sovereign risk, political risk, rule of law
> - Counterparty risk – level of guarantees on the offtake agreements
> - Commercial arrangements – whether there is an offtake agreement or full merchant exposure
> - Lifecycle of the asset – whether in development, under construction, or operational
>
> Masdar is primarily an equity investor. When structuring deals, Masdar seeks to maximise the use of long-term debt – and for such debt to be non-recourse to Masdar's balance sheet. In practical terms, this means that the lenders decide the amount of leverage, based on their criteria for coverage ratio.
>
> The equity provided by Mubadala, its only shareholder, allows Masdar to act as a long-term investor. Nonetheless, the company avoids investing in assets that it may not be able to exit, and sometimes divests assets. Reasons for divestment may include tactical optimisation of returns; strategic portfolio re-alignment; selling down to a strategic partner to share risk; or returning cash to its shareholder. Masdar has the flexibility to pursue a full or partial exit in a private transaction, or a full or partial exit from an investment vehicle marketed to a private group of investors or to the public markets. Market liquidity and Masdar's return expectations are the two potential constraints that affect its exit strategies.
>
> Source: Mohamed Jameel Al Ramahi, Chief Executive Officer of Masdar, and Masdar website.

Some sovereign funds have a limited allocation to unlisted infrastructure. The debate around the recent adjustment to the mandate of Norway's USD 1 trillion sovereign fund, the GPFG, provides an informative illustration of the issues facing sovereign funds that choose to diversify this way. As of 2020, the GFPG will be able to invest in unlisted renewable energy infrastructure. Initially, the Norwegian Parliament has allocated NOK 120 billion (Norwegian Krone) (USD 13 billion) for this purpose, or about 1.2% of the fund's capital. Ahead of the change, Norwegian and international climate-related NGOs were calling for a more significant role for the GPFG in climate finance. The government, on the other hand, emphasised the fund's fiduciary duty to maximise risk-adjusted returns. When it became increasingly clear that unlisted clean-energy infrastructure investments could generate competitive risk-adjusted returns, Norges Bank Investment Management (NBIM), which manages the GPFG, endorsed the diversification into unlisted infrastructure, which was approved by Parliament in 2019.

The climate impact of the GPFG's infrastructure investments, and that of other sovereign funds that diversify into infrastructure, will largely be determined by the extent to which sovereign funds decide to invest in new "greenfield" versus existing "brownfield" infrastructure. This is because the offer of greenfield infrastructure projects is inelastic. In other words, increased demand for existing "brownfield" infrastructure has limited effect on the supply of new projects. The reason for this is that most investors prefer de-risked brownfield infrastructure, which already generates revenue, rather than investing in the development and construction phases, which generally carry higher risk. In recent years, increased demand has therefore led to a significant rise in the prices of brownfield infrastructure, whereas the number of greenfield projects has remained steady (Plimmer, 2017[24]). To the extent that sovereign funds' investments are directed at brownfield infrastructure, these investments will contribute to further price increases and will have limited climate-related impact.

Sovereign funds that seek to invest in greenfield infrastructure could examine the precedents set by large pension funds that undertake this kind of investment. With the price of brownfield infrastructure assets going up, pension funds have found it increasingly difficult to get a good return on such investments. Several Canadian and Danish pension funds therefore seek higher returns in greenfield, where there is less competition (Box 3). However, as discussed in Section 5, infrastructure investment is highly skills-intensive, and would require extensive capacity building for sovereign funds that have been set up to invest in listed securities. This is particularly true for greenfield investment, which requires sector-specific knowledge and experience in engineering as well as in finance.

Box 3. Pension fund investment in a new clean-energy infrastructure

Very few pension funds invest directly in infrastructure, and even fewer undertake direct investment in new "greenfield" infrastructure. However, several large Canadian and Danish pension funds have developed the capacity for direct infrastructure investment, including clean energy and greenfield. These include for example the Ontario Teachers' Pension Plan. OTPP is a USD 150 billion pension fund that has its own greenfield team, but also does greenfield investment through joint project development platforms with others. The Caisse de Depots et Placements de Quebec (CDPQ) USD 230 billion) and Denmark's PKA (USD 48 billion) also make greenfield infrastructure investments. PKA, whose web page states "wind and sun provides good pensions", has nearly 10% of its capital invested in climate-related projects, of which about half in offshore wind farms.

The experience of these Canadian and Danish pension funds, and of Mubadala and Masdar (Box 2), demonstrates that it is possible for large institutional investors such as sovereign funds to develop the capacity to invest in greenfield infrastructure, either directly, through a SIF, or through joint investment platforms where several investors bring complementary capabilities.

Source: CPPIB, CDPQ, PKA and OTPP websites.

Sovereign funds

Asset level: Exclusion and divestment from inefficient high-carbon assets

Divestment targets high emission sectors such as coal mining and thermal power generation. The impact of divestment is controversial, since the divested companies can seek capital elsewhere. Unless the divestment leads to the high-carbon asset being closed down upon divestment, or its emissions significantly reduced, these emissions will continue. Many investors argue that engaging with portfolio companies to reduce their carbon footprint is likely to have a higher impact. In general, sovereign funds could see divestment as a last resort option, in cases where emissions-related engagement with portfolio companies has not worked.

The total value of documented divestment by sovereign funds is USD 2.9 billion (Capape, 2017[4]), or about 0.04% of the total value of assets held by sovereign funds. Norway's GPFG dominated these divestments; for a total value of USD 2.1 billion, followed by the New Zealand Superannuation Fund (NZSF) (USD 693 million).

The arguments for implementing these divestments were financial as much as political. For example, Norges Bank Investment Management (NBIM), which manages the GPFG, expects coal-based assets to continue losing value as countries step up efforts to address climate change. Therefore, NBIM has since 2016 excluded from its portfolio firms that derive more than 30% of their revenue from coal (Capape, 2017[4]). In the case of New Zealand, the divestments resulted from the implementation of its new global equity benchmark, which excludes carbon-intensive companies (Capapé and Santiváñez, 2017[2]). The NZSF aims to reduce the carbon emission intensity of its portfolio by at least 20% by 2020 and reduce the carbon reserves of the fund by at least 40%. To achieve this, it has sold stakes in almost 300 companies (Capape, 2017[4]).

Asset level: Engagement with portfolio companies

Like other investors, sovereign funds exercise their ownership role of portfolio companies through shareholder meetings and resolutions, and at board level in companies where they hold board seats. Investors that implement a climate-conscious ownership policy engage with portfolio companies on climate-related risks, emissions reductions and disclosure. Sovereign funds set up to track indexes are committed to allocating capital according to the index, and therefore do not have the option of investing in or divesting from companies according to their climate performance. For these sovereign funds, engagement is their only choice when seeking to implement climate-related objectives.

Sovereign funds differ in their capacity to exercise active ownership, and engaging directly with portfolio companies. Many sovereign funds do not have the capacity to exercise active ownership, and leave these responsibilities to their asset managers. One large sovereign fund, Norway's GPFG, has upon Parliament's request developed sophisticated policies for active ownership, which include not only economic, social, and governance matters, but also addresses climate-related risks of portfolio companies.

According to NBIM, the carbon footprint of NBIM's listed equity portfolio in 2015 was 12% less than its reference portfolio. In 2016, this figure increased to 16%, implying an improvement of 4 percentage points that year (Capape, 2017[4]); (Norges Bank Investment Management, 2016[25]). There are no independent studies to confirm a positive impact of NBIM's climate-related engagement with portfolio companies. However, recent research shows that NBIM's engagement on governance-related matters has led to better corporate governance of portfolio companies (Aguilera, R., et al., 2019[26]). This finding confirms the impact of NBIM's active ownership in general, and together with NBIM's own assessment provides an indication that NBIM's climate-related engagement with companies could also be impactful.

Asset manager level

There are currently no comprehensive studies of sovereign funds' climate-related engagement with asset managers. A recent study of pension funds (Asset Owners Disclosure Project, 2018[27]) shows that less than 40% of pension funds have factored climate change into their selection, monitoring and evaluation of asset managers. According to the same study, a minority of asset owners nevertheless do take leading positions on climate finance. In an example from a Dutch asset owner, the pension fund ABP developed a carbon budget for all portfolio companies, jointly with its primary asset manager. The carbon budget supports the achievement of a target of 25% reduction of CO_2 emission in their equity portfolio by 2020.

In its simplest form, sovereign funds' guidance for asset managers can include sector– and company exclusion criteria. For example, NBIM has since 2016 had specific sector restrictions for its external managers in relation to environmental, social and governance risks.

Process level

At the process level, sovereign funds and SIFs can be assessed by the extent to which their internal structures and processes take account of the implementation of climate-related objectives. No broad comprehensive assessment exists of the level of climate alignment of sovereign funds' structures and processes. However, sovereign funds' level of commitment to international frameworks for climate-alignment of investment processes, and the reporting of these processes, provides an important indication. Table 1 provides an overview of sovereign funds that have officially adhered to climate-relevant international initiatives.

As shown in the table, sovereign funds have limited adherence to international investor protocols on climate finance. Only two sovereign funds, the New Zealand Superannuation Fund and Norway's NBIM, are among the more than 1 000 supporters of the TCFD. The One Planet SWF Working Group has six sovereign funds as its founding members. The UN Principles for Responsible Investment has six sovereign funds and SIFs among its 2 500 members. No sovereign funds or SIF has yet joined the UN Portfolio Decarbonisation Coalition, although France's CDC, now part of BPIfrance, was a member.

Table 1. Sovereign fund and SIF participation in climate-related investor initiatives

Name of fund	Country	Sovereign fund/SIF	TCFD	One Planet	PRI
Total # of signatories			1 027[1]	6	2 500
ADIA	Abu Dhabi	Sovereign fund		✓	
BPIfrance	France	SIF			✓
InfraCredit	Nigeria	NSIA is founding shareholder			✓
ISIF	Ireland	SIF			✓
KIA	Kuwait	Sovereign fund		✓	
NZSF	New Zealand	Sovereign fund		✓	✓
NBIM	Norway	Sovereign fund	✓	✓	✓
Khazanah	Malaysia	SIF			✓
Ithmar Capital	Morocco	SIF			✓
PIF	Saudi Arabia	SIF		✓	
QIA	Qatar	Sovereign fund		✓	

Note: As of February 2020.
Source: TCFD, PRI, and One Planet SWF websites.

Strategic investment funds

Asset level: Direct investment, private capital mobilisation and portfolio company engagement

Contrary to sovereign funds, SIFs are mainly direct investors, and target specific sectors. This includes renewable energy and other infrastructure sectors. SIFs are set up to mobilise additional private investment – investment that would not have taken place without the SIF's involvement. SIFs do this by co-investing with private-sector partners, and by attracting private capital at the level of the SIF itself – at the fund level. Typical partners include project developers and private equity firms, with debt financing provided by banks and other debt providers. SIFs seek to supply financial products that are under-supplied by the market. For example, the equity markets of many developing countries are underdeveloped, and debt financing beyond 8-10 years maturity is frequently rare. SIFs can help fill these gaps. In other cases, it is the SIF's knowledge of the local market that makes it an attractive partner for foreign investors. Furthermore, private investors may perceive SIFs' connections to government as an implicit political risk guarantee, providing them with the necessary reassurance to invest.

A number of SIFs are investors in low-carbon infrastructure. Examples include the European Union's Marguerite Fund, which has 13 investments in solar, wind, biomass and energy-from-waste infrastructure across the European Union; the Ireland Strategic Investment Fund, which has invested in energy storage and in several private equity funds is focused on wind and other renewables; and Senegal's *Fonds Stratégiques d'Investissements (FONSIS)*, which has invested in solar energy in Senegal. SIFs have been successful at mobilising private capital, including from institutional investors (Halland, Noel and Tordo, 2016[10]).

In an interesting example of private capital mobilisation by a SIF, the Canadian Pension Plan Investment Board, and the Ontario Teachers' Pension Plan, as well as AustralianSuper, an Australian pension fund, in 2019 invested a total of USD 650 million in India's National Investment and Infrastructure Fund (NIIF) Master Fund, thereby bringing the Master Fund to its targeted size of USD 2.1 billion. Additionally, the three pension funds will have co-investment rights with the NIIF of a total of USD 1.95 billion. Whereas this investment is not meant for greenfield, and it is unclear how much of the capital will be allocated for low-carbon purposes, these investments do demonstrate the capacity of well-designed and well-run SIFs to mobilise capital from large institutional investors.

At least one SIF, Norway's recently established *Nysnø*, has been set up for the specific purpose of investing in low-carbon technology – including solar technology and sensor technology to support energy efficiency. *Nysnø* defines itself as a sovereign climate investment company and operates under the authority of the Norwegian Ministry of Trade, Industry and Fisheries. *Nysnø* is yet incipient, and has a very small portfolio consisting of five companies and two technology seed funds.[3] To be additional to private-sector financing, investments in low-carbon technology firms need to target financing gaps that are not covered by private-sector finance, including by acting as a venture financier for early-stage technology, where the private sector still perceives risk as being too high.

There is little information available on SIFs' engagement with portfolio companies. As direct investors, SIFs can seek to influence portfolio companies' climate-related activities without the need to go through intermediaries.

Intermediary level

Most SIFs do not make use of asset managers in the traditional sense, and there is little publicly available information on the climate-related engagement of SIFs with their intermediaries. Some SIFs, such as the EU Marguerite Fund, have established a dedicated management company that manages only the SIF's portfolio. In at least one case, the Philippine Investment Alliance for Infrastructure (PINAI), a private asset manager manages the SIF – in this case Macquarie Infrastructure and Real Assets.

In some cases, SIFs invest in other funds, taking the role of fund-of-funds. In these cases, the SIF typically provides a capped proportion of the total capitalisation of the funds that it invests in. SIFs have used this strategy particularly to finance small and medium-sized enterprises (SMEs), and for small or medium-sized infrastructure projects. For example, the Global Energy Efficiency and Renewable Energy Fund (GEEREF) is a multinational fund-of-funds advised by the European Investment Bank. GEEREF invests in private equity funds that focus on renewable energy and energy efficiency in emerging markets. India's NIIF has a fund-of-funds component that invests in Indian infrastructure-focused investment funds, which in turn invest in medium-sized infrastructure projects. Senegal's FONSIS invested in Teranga Capital, which in turn provides financing for SMEs.

Process level

There is little publicly available information on the level of climate alignment of SIFs' internal structures and processes. As of the time of writing, no SIFs are among the nearly 900 official supporters of the recommendations of the TCFD. Four SIFs are signatories to the PRI (Table 1).

Box 4. Low-carbon investment in the Silk Road Fund and Belt and Road initiative

The USD 40 billion Silk Road Fund (SRF), a "long-term development and investment fund" was established in 2014 by the Chinese government. The SRF was established to invest in the Beijing-led Belt and Road initiative, together with other public and private Chinese and international financial institutions. Given the SRF's important role in the financing of projects in the Belt and Road initiative, the climate-related policies and practices of the SRF could have an important impact on the emissions profile of these projects.

A recent study by Tsinghua University and Vivid Economies finds that the joint GHG emissions of the 126 Belt and Road countries could rise from 28% of the global total today, to 66% in 2050. According to the Study, "If B&RCs (Belt and Road countries) follow historical carbon-intense growth patterns... it may be enough to result in a 2.7 degree path, even if the rest of the world adheres to 2 degree levels of emissions." The Study calls for the decarbonisation of more than USD 12 trillion of planned infrastructure investments, and for safeguards to ensure the implementation of low-carbon technologies and practices.

The SRF is one of the 29 global institutions that are initial signatories to the Green Investment Principles for the Belt and Road (GIP), established in November 2018. The GIP are a set of voluntary principles jointly launched by the Green Finance Committee of the China Society for Finance and Banking, and the City of London. The initiative seeks the commitment of financial institutions and corporations that invest and operate in the Belt and Road region, to align their projects with environmental sustainability requirements and the Paris Agreement.

Source: (Ma Jun, 2019[28]), (OECD, 2018[29]) (Tsinghua University, Vivid Economics, 2019[30]).

5 How sovereign funds and SIFs can play a stronger role in the low-carbon transition

This section discusses the causes of sovereign funds' and SIFs' limited engagement with climate finance, and how barriers to engagement can be addressed for sovereign funds and SIFs to play a stronger role in the low-carbon transition. Sovereign funds and SIFs can also complement each other when seeking climate alignment. The section first considers sovereign funds, then SIFs, then the potential for synergies between these two types of state-sponsored investment funds.

Sovereign funds

The reforms required for sovereign funds to play a stronger role in the low-carbon transition are in part incumbent on governments that own sovereign funds; in part they concern sovereign funds themselves, and the role of their boards and management. Finally, some reforms relate to the role of sovereign funds' asset managers, advisers and other service providers.

Policy, mandate and strategy

Generally, sovereign funds' mandates emphasise the funds' fiduciary responsibility to the state and its citizens. The mandates stress sovereign funds' obligation to invest on commercial terms, seeking to maximise risk-adjusted returns. Sovereign funds' role as commercial investors is also enshrined in the Santiago Principles, and this unity of focus provides the funds' boards and management with clarity of objectives. If there is a real or perceived trade-off between a sovereign fund's fiduciary responsibility and climate considerations, the sovereign fund's board and management are then likely to prioritise the fiduciary responsibility. Sovereign funds' climate strategies therefore need to be consistent with their fiduciary responsibilities.

Sovereign funds implement the mandate given to them by their government owner, and are unlikely to alter their *modus operandi* on climate unless instructed to do so by their government. A decision to align a sovereign fund's activities with the low-carbon transition is therefore a political decision, rather than a technical one. Governments that wish their sovereign funds to align with the low-carbon transition therefore need to provide the fund with the foundations to do so. Governments can do this by establishing investment beliefs for their sovereign fund that are aligned with climate risk and climate impact. Arguably, governments could also include climate alignment in their sovereign fund's mandate, while retaining the characteristics of the sovereign fund as a commercial, profit-maximising investor organisation.

Sovereign fund boards could request fund management to define a strategy for climate alignment, based on the investment beliefs established by the government. The board could also ensure clarity in fund governance with regard to responsibilities for implementing alignment (Caldecott and Harnett, n.d.[13]).

Costs of climate alignment

Even when it makes financial sense, the integration of climate considerations has costs. These costs include those arising from training of staff, investments in new capabilities that the sovereign funds cannot easily build with current staffing, as well as the upgrading of governance structures, strategy, risk management, and other procedures. There are also recurrent costs, such as those associated with engaging with asset managers and portfolio companies on climate-related issues, costs of analysing portfolio companies' carbon footprint, and costs arising from additional efforts to implement climate-related reporting and disclosure. If a sovereign fund's climate alignment is underfunded, and incentives for management and staff are based on financial performance only, these additional activities may be perceived as onerous by the fund's board, management and investment teams. Governments that wish to climate-align their funds need to allow them the budgetary leeway to implement reforms.

Capability, governance and skills

In a survey of 22 leading asset owners, the Asset Owners Disclosure Project (Asset Owners Disclosure Project, 2018[23]) finds that successful climate strategies are underpinned by strong climate-related governance, and "buy-in" from trustees and senior management. Climate alignment requires clarity of responsibilities for climate-related issues at board and management level, as outlined in the recommendations of the TCFD, and overall climate-aligned governance. Few sovereign funds yet have this.

Climate alignment and "greenfield" infrastructure investment requires sector-specific skills and knowledge, not only in the area of finance but also in engineering. The very low share of low-carbon assets in sovereign fund portfolios is likely to be related to skills gaps in the areas of infrastructure investment and low-carbon technology. In fact, few sovereign funds possess these types of skills. While sovereign funds have diversified portfolios and objectives, funds that seek to undertake direct investment in low-carbon infrastructure need to build or acquire this capacity.

For large sovereign funds it may be viable to procure an existing infrastructure-focused asset manager that already has a track record. For sovereign funds that seek to increase their exposure to listed "green" infrastructure, or to invest in infrastructure-focused private equity funds, capacity requirements are lower than for direct investment (McKinsey&Company, 2016[31]). These funds will nonetheless need the staff and management capabilities required to understand the infrastructure sectors in which they will be investing. For sovereign funds that already invest in private markets, the skills acquired in these markets may be deployed for green investments (Capape, 2017[4]).

Climate-aligned engagement with portfolio companies also requires skills and resources. Among sovereign funds, Norway's NBIM has been a leader in building this type of capabilities. The use of climate criteria for the selection, monitoring and evaluation of asset managers requires capabilities that most sovereign funds have not yet developed.

Governments that seek to climate align their sovereign funds may request the sovereign fund's board and management to elaborate a plan and a budget for capacity building, consistent with the fund's climate strategy. Where needed, they could seek the support of external advisors. For investment in greenfield clean-energy infrastructure, the experience of Masdar suggests that expertise, but also strategy and partnerships are core elements that sovereign funds and their governments need to consider (Box 5).

Leveraging partnerships

While developing in-house capacity to operate as climate-aligned investors, sovereign funds can seek to bridge capability gaps through partnerships with organisations that have relevant complementary capabilities. Such partners may include service providers, equity investors, lenders, industry regulators and industry associations. Partnerships have been a core component of Masdar's strategy to develop the capabilities required for investing in greenfield clean-energy infrastructure (Box 5).

> **Box 5. Masdar's top three priorities for sovereign funds that consider investing in greenfield clean-energy infrastructure**
>
> Masdar sees strategy, expertise and partners as the three top priorities for sovereign funds that seek to invest in greenfield clean-energy infrastructure.
>
> - Strategy: Sovereign funds need to determine their strategy-and-return expectations early on. They need to define and understand their own competitive advantage, while tailoring business and operating models to maximise returns.
>
> - Expertise: It is critical to recruit and retain the right talent, while utilising external service providers to deliver for those parts of the business that are more commoditised. It is also vital to incentivise staff properly to deliver – especially investment managers. Masdar has benefited from being a specialist investor: as it invests only in renewables and sustainable real estate, it can focus on recruiting in-house expertise to target those sectors. To mitigate the risk of knowledge erosion due to employee turnover, Masdar cultivates human capital. It prioritises the employment of young graduates, particularly United Arab Emirates (UAE) nationals, and seeks to fast-track their development.
>
> - Partners: It is crucial to select partners that add value; you need to build an extensive network among suppliers, equity investors, lenders, regulators, industry associations, and other potential partners. Rather than expanding prematurely, and risk overreaching, leverage partnerships to get to where you want to be.
>
> Source: *Mohamed Jameel Al Ramahi, Chief Executive Officer of Masdar.*

Concerns about returns

A frequent concern for institutional investors that seek to climate align their portfolios is whether this is compatible with their fiduciary duty to maximise returns (Asset Owners Disclosure Project, 2018[27]), 2018a, (Capape, 2017[4]). Sovereign funds' commercial orientation does not necessarily preclude the funds from playing a role as instruments of climate policy. There is a growing body of evidence that climate-aligned investment generates competitive returns. For example, one study finds that long-term passive investors such as sovereign funds may hedge climate risk without sacrificing financial returns. Sovereign funds can do this by investing in a decarbonised index based on a standard benchmark, such as the Standard & Poor's 500 index, while minimising the tracking error with respect to the underlying benchmark. The authors note that decarbonised indices have so far matched or even outperformed benchmark indices, because financial markets still tend to under-price carbon risk (Andersson, Bolton and Samama, 2016[32]). Another study (IEA and Imperial College, 2020) finds that renewable power outperforms fossil fuels in US and European markets. The study found that clean power stocks generated higher returns than stocks in fossil fuel companies over the past ten years, five years, and one year. Whereas US renewable power stocks generated an average annual return of 11.4% from 2010 to 2019, fossil fuel stocks had an average return of 7% during the same period. (International Energy Agency and Imperial College Business School, Centre for Climate and Investment, 2020[33]). A third study, by data provider Morningstar, finds that the six out of ten sustainable funds delivered higher returns than equivalent conventional funds over the past decade, and weather downturns better (Riding, n.d.[34])).

A recent assessment of the world's largest 100 pension funds finds that the most climate-aligned funds have 6% allocation to low-carbon solutions (Asset Owners Disclosure Project, 2018[27]). This indicates that it is possible for institutional investors, including sovereign funds, to increase their allocation to low-carbon, without compromising returns.

Incorporation of climate alignment into external management contracts and incentives

In theory, sovereign funds would be able to establish a set of incentives for asset managers to act as long-term investors, and consistently with the financial, climate, and ESG objectives of the fund. In practice, sovereign funds and other institutional investors assess managers largely based on quarterly results, and it has proved challenging to define management contract terms that incentivise investment with a long-term horizon. In addition to having different time horizons, asset managers and asset owners also have different perceptions of the importance of environmental issues. Research shows that, given the case of a profitable company whose activities are damaging the environment, only 19% of asset managers would pull their money out, whereas 38% of asset owners would do so (Schroders, 2016[35]) (Capape, 2017[4]).

Sovereign funds should seek to select, monitor and evaluate asset managers based on defined climate-related criteria, and could establish carbon reduction targets for asset managers. To enhance the climate performance of asset managers, climate-conscious sovereign funds should seek to provide asset managers with incentives for capital allocation to well performing low-carbon, long-term assets. For sovereign funds to exercise effective oversight of asset managers' climate performance, these asset managers must be transparent about climate-related aspects of their management practices. However, asset managers frequently apply a "black box" policy, by considering as proprietary knowledge their climate-related procedures and performance indicators for managing portfolio companies. Asset managers do not necessarily share their methodologies with asset owners such as sovereign funds.

Perceptions of lack of low-carbon investment opportunities

Amongst investors, a frequently cited reason for limited climate engagement is a perceived lack of low-carbon investment opportunities. This perceived lack of opportunities reflects a "static" view of carbon-related aspects of portfolio management, as well as insufficient investor capability to develop new low-carbon assets – particularly in the infrastructure sectors.

First, sovereign funds' climate performance should be assessed not only "statically", based on the share of low-carbon assets in their portfolio, but also "dynamically", based on the emissions reduction of firms in the portfolio. If sovereign funds see companies with potential for emissions reduction as low-carbon investment opportunities, then there should be no lack of such opportunities. Sovereign funds could then exercise climate-aligned active ownership of companies, and pursue portfolio-wide targets for emissions reduction. The implementation of such targets by sovereign funds should include the definition of clear expectations for portfolio companies, with regard to climate-related risk as well as impact; active engagement with these companies; as well as the integration of climate risk management into company and asset valuations (Caldecott and Harnett, n.d.[13]).

Second, in the infrastructure sectors there is strong demand for operating assets. However, high risk at the development and construction stages has kept this demand from translating into additional projects. In other words, new infrastructure has a low price-elasticity of supply. With private investors competing for operational infrastructure assets and pushing up the price of these assets, sovereign funds' investment in operational infrastructure would make little difference to climate finance beyond contributing to a further increase in the price of the assets.

The example of Masdar and of Canadian pension funds (Boxes 2 and 3), shows that it is feasible for an institutional investor such as a sovereign fund to develop new infrastructure projects. To gain access to new low-carbon infrastructure assets, sovereign funds could establish or invest in project development companies such as Masdar, they could set up infrastructure investment platforms jointly with other institutional investors, or they could in-source their direct investment management functions for infrastructure. Several large institutional investors have in-sourced investment management, thereby not only strengthening their capacity to invest in long-term assets such as infrastructure, but also eliminating management fees (Singh Bachher, Dixon and Monk, 2017[11]).

Lack of reliable climate-related data

A main challenge when seeking to assess sovereign funds' climate-related activities is the scarcity of publicly available information. Sovereign fund transaction databases, such as that of the Sovereign Wealth Fund Institute (SWFI), do not include data on climate-related aspects of deals – which sovereign funds in any case generally do not report. Transaction level analysis therefore has to be undertaken in an ad-hoc manner, based on criteria for climate relevance that are not used by sovereign funds themselves in their reporting (OECD, 2016[36]).

Scarcity of climate-related information is a challenge not only with regard to sovereign fund transactions, but also with respect to their internal processes. According to the Asset Owners Disclosure Project, only eight sovereign funds currently disclose publicly their strategies on climate change. Of these eight, only three are based in emerging markets and developing economies. Furthermore, with the exception of Azerbaijan, Norway and UAE, asset owners in fossil fuel producing countries, including sovereign funds, "consistently rank lowest for climate risk disclosure" (Asset Owners Disclosure Project, 2018[37]). Finally, among the more than 1 000 organisations that support the recommendations of the Task Force on Climate-Related Financial Disclosures (TCFD), including some of the world's largest investment banks, insurance companies, asset managers and institutional investors, there are only two sovereign funds – the New Zealand Superannuation Fund and Norway's GPFG.

The lack of available information is compounded by relatively lax financial reporting requirements in many emerging markets; by joint deals in private markets where a sovereign fund is one of several investors, and due to the challenges of tracing sovereign fund capital that is invested through third-party asset managers (Capape, 2017[4]). A minority of sovereign funds, such as Norway's GPFG and the New Zealand Superannuation Fund, operate with a high level of transparency.

The lack of climate-related reporting by sovereign funds mirrors insufficiencies in climate-related reporting by portfolio companies. Although many companies have made progress on climate-related disclosure and reporting, the information published by most companies on climate risk and climate impact remains insufficient for investors to take informed decisions (Task Force on Climate-Related Financial Disclosures, 2019[38]).

There are several reasons for sovereign funds' general reluctance to publish information on their practices and transactions, including climate-related aspects. Many sovereign funds consider, like other commercial investors, that their investment practices and decisions are reflective of proprietary knowledge and skills. They may see transparency coming at a cost, since information revealed may be of use to competitors. Nonetheless, increased transparency is in principle no less achievable to sovereign funds than to the numerous other large investment organisations that have chosen to join the TCFD. To start a process towards climate alignment of sovereign funds, governments could instruct their sovereign funds to join other major financial institutions in reporting according to the recommendations of the TCFD. Sovereign funds that remain uncomfortable with disaggregated public reporting on their activities could, at second best, report publicly on aggregate low-carbon investments, while reserving the full reporting for their government owners (Capape, 2017[4]).

Sovereign funds could in turn drive visibility on climate-related information by requesting their asset managers and portfolio firms to adhere to the recommendations of the TCFD. In particular, in private markets, which are frequently opaque, sovereign funds could have an important role in driving visibility on climate-related variables. In the last instance, sovereign funds could divest from firms that, after sustained engagement, refuse to pursue disclosure standards consistent with the recommendations of the TCFD. In an analogy to financial reporting, few investors would hesitate to divest from a company that does not publish financial statements consistent with the International Financial Reporting Standards (IFRS) or other accepted accounting standards.

Cultural obstacles and lack of incentives

Many investors or trustees regard climate change as an ethical or political issue rather than a financial one (Asset Owners Disclosure Project, 2018[23]). To overcome this kind of obstacle, sovereign funds may need to offer board members, managers, and staff training on climate risk, climate impact and climate-aligned investment practices.

A lack of incentives for climate-related performance, at the board, management, and staff level, is likely to be an important cause of sovereign funds' inaction on climate. Governments may need to establish incentive structures for fund management that are consistent with climate objectives, or mandate the fund's board to establish such incentive structures.

Regulatory environment and other external factors

Sovereign funds' climate-related engagement is affected by external factors that have a broad impact on investors, such as a lack of momentum in climate-relevant regulation and policy, unstable infrastructure and clean-energy investment regimes, and the unpredictability of investing in fast-evolving technology sectors. In emerging markets, investment may be further complicated by weak rule of law, lack of information for due diligence, currency risk and political risk. Emerging markets may provide attractive opportunities in terms of returns, portfolio diversification and climate impact, yet these markets require the investor to be able to accept and mitigate the associated higher risk.

Few national regulators have so far integrated climate-related disclosure and reporting broadly into their national regulatory frameworks. Such reporting and disclosure is therefore still largely voluntary. This includes, for example, the recommendations of the TCFD, as well as the recently approved EU Taxonomy and the EU Green Bonds Index (see discussion in Box 6 below). The incorporation of relevant voluntary frameworks into national regulation, in particular the recommendations of the TCFD and the Taxonomy, would have an important effect on sovereign funds' climate-related disclosure and reporting.

Given their size, influence and connection to government, sovereign funds could provide crucial support for the development of climate-related financial regulations. (Asset Owners Disclosure Project, 2018[23]) (2018b) calls on regulators to clarify legal duties with respect to "integrating climate-related aspects in decision making, install mandatory reporting requirements in line with the TCFD recommendations, and support the development of a harmonised taxonomy for low-carbon investments". Sovereign funds could support the implementation of this kind of regulatory reforms.

> **Box 6. Consolidation of climate-related reporting and classification standards**
>
> The lack of a generally accepted framework or standards on climate-related reporting and classification has been a significant hindrance to the broad adoption of climate-relevant investment practices. This includes common standards to describe the climate-relevant characteristics of economic activities, assets and financial products. Until recently, NGOs and industry organisations have produced a diversity of climate finance classification and reporting frameworks, whereas official standard setting bodies and regulators have been lagging behind.
>
> This has meant that investors lack clarity of what constitutes a "green" investment, which has muddied the waters for asset owners and managers that wish to green their practices and portfolios, and has increased the risk of "greenwashing" of assets – the practice of reporting assets as "greener" than they actually are. The lack of generally accepted standards has also made it difficult to compare the climate

performance of firms, asset managers and asset owners, and has probably translated into less pressure on asset owners and asset managers to disclose their climate-related activities.

A process of consolidation is currently taking place, whereby intergovernmental bodies are getting more involved in the consolidation of climate finance reporting and classification frameworks.

First, the Recommendations of the Task Force on Climate-Related Financial Disclosures (TCFD, 2017[39]), established by the Financial Stability Board, constitutes a milestone for defining climate-related disclosures. The TCFD recommends disclosures in the areas of governance, strategy, risk management, and metrics and targets. More specifically, this means that companies should report on (1) the role of the board and management in the company's response to climate change; (2) how strategic planning takes climate change into account; (3) the integration of climate risk in risk management procedures; and (4) performance against indicators that are based on the company's climate strategy and risk management.

Second, there has been important progress towards establishing a generally applicable standard of environmentally sustainable economic activities and assets. The European Union's Taxonomy for environmentally sustainable activities seeks to fill this gap, albeit on a voluntary basis. The framework, which was agreed in December 2019 by the European Council and the European Parliament, is expected to come into force by the end of 2021. China proposed a taxonomy for green finance in 2013, and other jurisdictions have also adopted legislative standards for financial products.

Third, consolidation is also taking place in the green bonds space. In 2015, China introduced the Green Bond Endorsed Project Catalogue, the world's first official standard for green bonds. The European Union is currently in the process of establishing an EU Green Bonds standard.

The consolidation of reporting frameworks represents an opportunity for sovereign funds that seek to implement climate-aligned disclosure and reporting, since it provides sovereign funds with clearly defined standards to align with.

Sources: (TCFD, 2017[39]), (EU Technical Expert Group on Sustainable Finance, 2019[40]).

Strategic investment funds

Many of the obstacles to climate-aligned investment that sovereign funds face are not relevant to SIFs. Several SIFs have a mandate to invest in green infrastructure and already assume related costs. As investors focus mainly on real assets, SIFs seek from the outset to be equipped with the capabilities necessary to invest directly in the sectors of their interest. Since most SIFs do not invest through intermediaries, they do not face principal-agent challenges when deploying capital, and SIFs frequently develop new infrastructure projects rather than seeking attractive investment opportunities in operational infrastructure. Since SIFs tend to invest significant minority shares, they have the leverage to push for portfolio companies' reporting of climate-relevant data, and as "double bottom line" investors, they consider non-financial as well as financial results.

For SIFs, a main challenge is to find the right balance between commercial and policy-driven investment, to manage the "double bottom line". An SIF with an excessively commercial orientation risks providing capital for investments that the private sector would have undertaken anyway – crowding out rather than crowding in private capital, and therefore providing little additionality. Conversely, an SIF with an excessively policy-determined *modus operandi* risks straying into the domain of non-commercial expenditures, which is the prerogative of government budgets (Gelb, Tordo and Halland, 2014[9]) (Halland, Noel and Tordo, 2016[10]).

SIFs' commercial orientation is what disciplines their investment process. It also provides them with necessary integrity vis-à-vis private sector partners. This commercial orientation is therefore a main foundation of their capacity to mobilise capital from private investors (OECD, 2019[7]). At the same time, SIFs exist to provide financial sector functions that the private sector would not provide by itself. In general terms, SIFs address this duality of purpose at four different levels: mandate, governance, skills and private sector orientation (Halland, Noel and Tordo, 2016[10]).

Mandate

SIFs are commonly set up to operate as commercial investors within a specific mandate. For example, the European Union's Marguerite Fund invests exclusively in early-stage infrastructure. Within this mandate, however, the fund operates as a commercial, profit-maximising investor and is managed by a private, partner-owned investment management company.

Governance

SIFs differ significantly with regard to their legal status and governance structure. However, each type of legal and governance structure seeks in a different way to insulate the SIFs commercial investment decisions from its government owner, and from political influence in general. This can be done, for example, by setting the SIF up under standard legislation for private equity funds, and establishing a private company to manage the SIF, as is the case for Marguerite. In the case of India's National Investment and Infrastructure Fund (NIIF), the Indian government owns a minority 49% of the fund, and has only two representatives on the fund's seven-person board. Like Marguerite, the NIIF is established under standard legislation for investment funds. The Ireland Strategic Investment Fund (ISIF) is part of the National Treasury Management Agency, a government agency, but its governance and decision-making framework contains a number of safeguards to enhance the commercial orientation of the fund.

Skills

SIFs take their genealogy from private equity funds, and recruit their board members, management and staff primarily from the private sector. For example, the Nigeria Sovereign Investment Authority (NSIA), which combines the functions of a sovereign fund and an SIF through its three sub-funds, has a board consisting entirely of representatives recruited from the private sector. Similarly, the NSIA recruits its management and staff from the private financial sector, and several senior executives recruited from the Nigerian diaspora have gained experience in global financial centres such as the City of London, Wall Street and Dubai.

Private sector orientation

The participation of private capital, either at the level of the SIF itself (at the fund level), or at the project level helps ensure that the SIF operates on commercial terms. Another benefit of private sector participation is that private co-investors can bring capacity and skills to due diligence and other aspects of the investment process.

As an example, when the Indian government set up the NIIF, it intentionally established the entity that would manage it, NIIF Limited, as a company rather than as a government agency. The purpose was to enhance the independence of the NIIF's investment decisions from political interference, and emphasise NIIF Limited's role as a commercial investment manager. Investors in the NIIF Master Fund are entitled to an equivalent ownership share in NIIF Limited, and investors representing more than 10% of the NIIF Master Fund's capital are entitled to board seats at NIIF Limited (NIIFIndia, 2020[41]; TCFD, 2017[39]).

Collaboration between sovereign funds and SIFs: Harnessing their potential for enhanced climate finance and action

The complementarities between sovereign funds and SIFs present opportunities for creating productive synergies between these two types of investment funds. As discussed above, sovereign funds hold very large amounts of capital, invested in different types of securities, while having limited capabilities for infrastructure investment, and for direct investment. SIFs, on the other hand, are small compared to sovereign funds, and are set up for direct investment, most commonly in infrastructure and SMEs. Many SIFs have the capabilities needed for investing in the development and construction of new infrastructure. This is a capacity that nearly all sovereign funds lack, with the exception of Abu Dhabi's Mubadala Investment Company, through its subsidiary Masdar (Box 2).

To take advantage of these complementarities for investment in low-carbon infrastructure, sovereign funds could channel part of their capital through SIFs, or they could set up joint investment platforms with SIFs. The investments of Temasek, Ontario Teachers', the Canada Pension Plans Investment Board, and AustralianSuper into India's NIIF, discussed above, confirm that it can be attractive for large institutional investors to provide capital for a specialised national infrastructure investor. Furthermore, institutional investors, including several large Canadian pension funds, are increasingly collaborating on direct investment, particularly in the infrastructure sectors (Box 3). Working through co-investment platforms allows them to pool resources and expertise to co-invest, while taking advantage of different partners' informational and/or geographical advantages (Singh Bachher, Dixon and Monk, 2017[11]).

There are several benefits to this kind of collaboration. First, sovereign funds can take advantage of SIFs' knowledge of their home markets, and ability to identify and monitor projects on the ground. Second, collaboration with SIFs can strengthen sovereign funds' deal flow, since the SIF as a local partner can identify, source and validate investment projects that sovereign funds may otherwise find it difficult to access. Third, collaboration with SIFs provides sovereign funds with opportunities for diversification. Fourth, collaboration allows sovereign funds and SIFs to share the costs of due diligence, research and monitoring. Fifth, collaboration through a joint platform allows for bypassing conventional intermediaries, thereby retaining governance rights and more direct control of investments. Sixth, as local partners SIFs can minimise headline risk and mitigate political risk. (Singh Bachher, Dixon and Monk, 2017[11]) provide a detailed discussion of these aspects of collaboration among institutional investors.

6 Conclusions

Sovereign funds differ widely in terms of their climate consciousness, and their climate-related transparency and disclosure practices. Sovereign funds' engagement with climate change remains, with a few notable exceptions, aspirational. Currently, sovereign funds as a group play a very small role in green finance. This publication argues that sovereign funds could become essential contributors to the low-carbon transition, without necessarily compromising their role as commercial investors. The observation that a minority of climate-conscious pension funds allocate up to 6% of their capital to low-carbon solutions indicates that it is possible for institutional investors to engage with the low-carbon transition while remaining on commercial terms and respecting fiduciary duties to shareholders (Asset Owners Disclosure Project, 2018[23]). As the global green investment agenda gains further traction, and as pressure builds on investors to "green" their portfolios, transparent and climate-conscious funds such as these could help build initial momentum. Over time, traditionally less climate-conscious sovereign funds might find it in their interest to join them (OECD, 2016[36]).

Importantly, the climate alignment of portfolios and of investment organisations such as sovereign funds and SIFs is increasingly becoming good business. Several studies indicate that climate-aligned portfolios can provide competitive returns. Moreover, it is part of sovereign funds' and SIFs' fiduciary duty to their citizens and government to take full account of climate risk in their operations.

Sovereign funds and other institutional investors frequently cite a lack of low-carbon investment opportunities as a challenge when seeking to climate-align their portfolios. Portfolio climate alignment should be seen as a dynamic process, where reducing the emissions of carbon-inefficient portfolio companies may count as much toward emissions reduction objectives as buying shares of companies that are already carbon efficient. Furthermore, high-capacity sovereign funds could seek to build the capabilities required for developing new low-carbon assets, as Mubadala does through its subsidiary Masdar.

To achieve higher allocations to green, sovereign funds would need to undertake major investments in capacity building across several areas. This includes i) capacity to engage with portfolio companies on climate-related issues; ii) capacity to select and monitor asset managers based on their climate-related performance, as well as – for the stronger sovereign funds – iii) capacity to invest directly in low-carbon infrastructure.

SIFs can contribute to the low-carbon transition by providing equity and other forms of investment capital to sectors and stages of the investment process where the private sector does not invest by itself (OECD, 2016[21]). However, although SIFs are a promising type of instrument for climate finance, and are becoming increasingly common across the world, these funds would need far larger amounts of capital to contribute meaningfully to the low-carbon transition.

Sovereign funds and SIFs are complementary in several ways, and the synergies between them could be further exploited. Sovereign funds could benefit from collaborating more closely with SIFs that already have many of the skills required for a role in climate finance, and with pension funds that have built the capacity for direct infrastructure investment. For SIFs, collaboration with sovereign funds would provide an opportunity to scale their investments in low-carbon infrastructure and other climate-related assets.

For these transformations to happen, sovereign funds and SIFs would need the guidance and support of their governments. Governments that wish for their sovereign funds and SIFs to manage climate-related risk better, and take a more active role in the low-carbon transition, need to establish strategies for this transformation, with concrete plans for implementation. If not being provided with a clear direction by their government and private sector owners, sovereign funds and SIFs are unlikely to drive change on their own. Furthermore, governments should require their sovereign funds and SIFs to report according to the standards of the TCFD, and seek to adopt internationally recognised standards for green assets and financial products. Sovereign funds that are reluctant to report publicly on their investments could disclose aggregate numbers on low-carbon investments.

Notes

[1] This document uses the term of *sovereign fund*. The term of *sovereign wealth fund* is also commonly used. The two terms are here treated as identical.

[2] For a definition of SIFs, see (Halland, Noel and Tordo, 2016[10]).

[3] As of May 2020.

References

Aguilera, R., et al. (2019), "Firms' reaction to changes in the governance preferences of active institutional owners", *Finance Working Paper*, No. 625/2019, European Corporate Governance Institute, https://papers.ssrn.com/sol3/papers.cfm?abstract_id=3411566. [26]

Andersson, M., P. Bolton and F. Samama (2016), "Hedging Climate Risk", *Financial Analyst's Journal*, Vol. 72/3, https://tandfonline.com/doi/10.2469/faj.v72.n3.4. [32]

Asset Owners Disclosure Project (2018), *Global Climate Index 2017*, https://aodproject.net/wp-content/uploads/2017/04/AODP-GLOBAL-INDEX-REPORT-2017_FINAL_VIEW.pdf. [37]

Asset Owners Disclosure Project (2018), *Pensions in a changing climate*, https://aodproject.net/changing-climate/. [23]

Asset Owners Disclosure Project (2018), *Winning Climate Strategies: Practical Solutions and Building Blocks for Asset Owners from Beginner to Best Practice*, https://aodproject.net/wp-content/uploads/2018/06/AODP-WinningStrategiesReport.pdf. [27]

Bloomberg NEF (2019), *New Energy Outlook 2019*, https://about.bnef.com/new-energy-outlook/. [20]

BNP Paribas (2019), *Wells, Wires and Wheels: Eroci and the Tough Road Ahead for Oil*, BNP Paribas Asset Management, https://docfinder.bnpparibas-am.com/api/files/1094E5B9-2FAA-47A3-805D-EF65EAD09A7F. [15]

Caldecott, B. (2018), *Stranded Assets and the Environment: Risk, resilience, and opportunity*, Routledge, https://www.routledge.com/Stranded-Assets-and-the-Environment-Risk-Resilience-and-Opportunity/Caldecott-Steiner-Stern/p/book/9781138120600. [14]

Caldecott, B. and E. Harnett (n.d.), "One Planet Sovereign Wealth Funds: Turning Ambition into Action", https://www.smithschool.ox.ac.uk/research/sustainable-finance/publications/One-Planet-Sovereign-Wealth-Funds-Turning-Ambition-into-Action.pdf. [13]

Capape, J. (2017), "Financing Sustainable Development: The Role of Sovereign Wealth Funds for Green Investment", UNEP, http://www.greenfiscalpolicy.org/wp-content/uploads/2018/05/SWF-Final-Study.pdf. [4]

Capapé, J. and M. Santiváñez (2017), *Sovereign Wealth Funds: Sustainable and active investors? The case of Norway*, https://sites.tufts.edu/sovereignet/files/2018/06/SustainableActiveInvestors_Capape.pdf. [2]

Carney, M. (2016), *Resolving the climate paradox*, BIS Central Bankers Speeches, http://www.berkshirehathaway.com/letters/letters.html. [16]

Carney, M. (2015), *Breaking the tragedy of the horizon-climate change and financial stability*, BIS Central Bankers Speeches, http://www.pwc.com/gx/en/ceo-agenda/ceo-survey.html. [12]

EU Technical Expert Group on Sustainable Finance (2019), *Taxonomy technical report*, European Union, https://ec.europa.eu/info/sites/info/files/business_economy_euro/banking_and_finance/documents/190618-sustainable-finance-teg-report-taxonomy_en.pdf. [40]

Gelb, Tordo and Halland (2014), *Sovereign Wealth Funds and Long-Term Development Finance: Risks and Opportunities*, World Bank, https://papers.ssrn.com/sol3/papers.cfm?abstract_id=2394324. [9]

Halland, H., M. Noel and S. Tordo (2016), "Strategic Investment Funds: Opportunities and Challenges", *World Bank Policy Research Working Paper Series*, No. 7851, World Bank, http://documents.worldbank.org/curated/en/235311475681523659/Strategic-investment-funds-opportunities-and-challenges. [10]

International Energy Agency and Imperial College Business School, Centre for Climate and Investment (2020), *Energy Investing: Exploring Risk and Return in the Capital Markets*, https://imperialcollegelondon.app.box.com/s/c2nj02f7apdz16tjw48y0kytdsutjq75. [33]

International Forum of Sovereign Wealth Funds (2019), *IFSWF Annual Review 2018*, https://www.ifswfreview.org/. [22]

Ma Jun (2019), *Greening the Belt and Road is essential to our climate's future*, World Economic Forum, https://www.weforum.org/agenda/2019/07/belt-and-road-climate-future-change-green/. [28]

McKinsey&Company (2016), "Unlisted Infrastructure Investments", *External review of Political, Regulatory, and Reputational Risks*, p. 35, https://www.regjeringen.no/contentassets/312e6001471045cc80be9b86b1fdae4d/risks_in_unlisted_infrastructure.pdf. [31]

NIIFIndia (2020), *NIIFIndia*, https://niifindia.in/. [41]

Norges Bank Investment Management (2016), *Responsible Investment Government Pension Fund Global*. [25]

OECD (2019), *Global Outlook on Financing for Sustainable Development 2019. Time to Face the Challenge.*, OECD, https://www.oecd.org/dac/financing-sustainable-development/development-finance-topics/Global-Outlook-on-Financing-for-SD-2019.pdf. [19]

OECD (2019), "Using extractive revenues for sustainable development: Policy guidance for resource-rich countries.", *OECD Policy Dialogue on Natural Resource Based Development.*, https://www.oecd.org/publications/using-extractive-revenues-for-sustainable-development-a9332691-en.htm. [8]

OECD (2019), *Using Extractives Revenues for Sustainable Development: Policy Guidance for Resource-Rich Countries*, OECD, https://www.oecd.org/publications/using-extractive-revenues-for-sustainable-development-a9332691-en.htm. [7]

OECD (2018), *Business and Finance Outlook 2018*, OECD, https://www.oecd-ilibrary.org/finance-and-investment/oecd-business-and-finance-outlook-2018_9789264298828-en. [29]

OECD (2018), *Making Blended Finance Work for the Sustainable Development Goals*, OECD Publishing, Paris, https://dx.doi.org/10.1787/9789264288768-en. [17]

OECD (2016), *Progress report on approaches to mobilizing institutional investment for green infrastructure*, OECD, http://unepinquiry.org/wp-content/uploads/2016/09/11_Progress_Report_on_Approaches_to_Mobilising_Institutional_Investment_for_Green_Infrastructure.pdf. [21]

OECD (2016), *Progress report on approaches to mobilizing institutional investment for green infrastructure*. [42]

OECD (2016), *Strategic Investment Funds: Comparative Analysis and Lessons Learned.*, Discussion paper presented at the Policy Dialogue on Natural Resource-Based Development. Unpublished. [36]

Ossowski, R. and H. Halland (2016), *Fiscal Management in Resource-Rich Countries: Essentials for Economists, Public Finance Professionals, and Policy Makers*, World Bank, https://openknowledge.worldbank.org/handle/10986/24577. [5]

Plimmer, G. (2017), "Investment in infrastructure assets soars to record", *Financial Times*, https://www.ft.com/content/c841e854-d988-11e6-944b-e7eb37a6aa8e. [24]

Riding, S. (n.d.), *Majority of ESG funds outperform wider market over 10 years*, https://www.ft.com/content/733ee6ff-446e-4f8b-86b2-19ef42da3824. [34]

Schroders (2016), *Global investor study: What investors think about responsible investing*, https://www.sustainablefinance.ch/upload/cms/user/SchrodersGlobalInvestmentStudy_nachhaltigesInvestieren_En.pdf. [35]

Singh Bachher, J., A. Dixon and A. Monk (2017), *The New frontier investors. How pension funds, sovereign wealth funds, and endowments are changing the busniess of invetment and long-term*, Palgrave, https://www.palgrave.com/gp/book/9781137508560. [11]

Sovereign Wealth Fund Institute (2020), *Sovereign Wealth Fund Rankings*, https://www.swfinstitute.org/fund-rankings/. [1]

Task Force on Climate-Related Financial Disclosures (2019), *2019 Status Report*, https://www.fsb-tcfd.org/publications/tcfd-2019-status-report/. [38]

TCFD (2017), *Recommendations of the Task Force on Climate-related Financial Disclosures*, Task Force on Climate-Related Financial Disclosures, https://www.fsb-tcfd.org/wp-content/uploads/2017/06/FINAL-2017-TCFD-Report-11052018.pdf. [39]

Tsinghua University, Vivid Economics, C. (2019), *Decarbonizing the Belt and Road Initiative: A green finance roadmap*, https://www.climateworks.org/wp-content/uploads/2019/09/Decarbonizing-the-Belt-and-Road_report_final_lo-res.pdf. [30]

UNCTAD (2014), *World Investment Report 2014. Investing in the SDGs: An Action Plan*, https://unctad.org/en/PublicationsLibrary/wir2014_en.pdf. [18]

van den Bremer, T. and F. van der Ploeg (2013), "Managing and harnessing volatile oil windfalls", *IMF Economic Review*, http://dx.doi.org/10.1057/imfer.2013.4. [6]

WillisTowersWatson (2019), *Global Pension Assets Study 2019*, https://www.willistowerswatson.com/en-GB/Insights/2019/02/global-pension-assets-study-2019. [3]

www.ingramcontent.com/pod-product-compliance
Lightning Source LLC
LaVergne TN
LVHW062000070526
838199LV00060B/4216